MY NAME IS MICHAEL

Learn How to Say My Name in 10 Languages

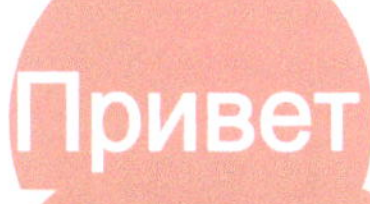

MY NAME IS MICHAEL

Learn How to Say My Name in 10 Languages

Written by:
Rufus and Jenny Triplett

Illustrated by:
Creative Azim

Another Dawah International, LLC Publication

Concept by: Rufus & Jenny Triplett ©2023
Dawah International, LLC,
a Multimedia Company/Rufus & Jenny Triplett

Library of Congress Cataloged - In Publication Data ISBN:
978-0-9979725-5-9 Dawah International, LLC Publishing

Dawah International, LLC Publishing PO Box 380
Powder Springs, GA 30127 678-389-2646
dawahinternationalllc@gmail.com

For Worldwide Distribution. Printed in the
United States of America.

Dedication

This book is dedicated in memory of our oldest
son Michael Triplett. An aspiring world traveler.

We also publish this with love to our other two
sons, Mosi and Miles.

We raised our boys to know that there
was a whole world outside of their block and life
was waiting for them to discover it.

5

Introduction

WELCOME to a book of discovery.

You will enjoy reading this book over and over again while being introduced to new languages from around the world.

To the child that reads this book, may your life be filled with adventure and discovery.

To the parent that reads with their child, may you enjoy the adventure as well as the education.

- Rufus and Jenny Triplett

My name is
Michael.

Statue of Liberty
New York City, NY
MY - Kull
Say my name
in English.

My name
is Miguel.

SOMBRERO
ME - Gell
Say my name
in Spanish.

My name is
Michael.

EIFFEL TOWER
PARIS, FRANCE
ME - Shell
Say my name
in French.

My name is
Mika'il.

ME - ki - eel
HOLY KAABA
MECCA, SAUDI ARABIA
Say my name
in Arabic.

My name is
Michael.

Mi - ke - er
Say my name in Mandarin.
FORBIDDEN CITY
BEIJING, CHINA

18

The 20 Most Spoken Languages in the World As Per Wikipedia

1. **English** - The most widely spoken language in the world > one billion.

2. **Mandarin** - The language with the most native speakers > one billion.

3. **Hindi** - Native to India. Almost 700 million speakers.

4. **Spanish** - The official language of Spain. Over 500 million speakers.

5. **French** - The language or art and culture. Over 300 million speakers.

6. **Arabic** - A beautiful language with unique pronunciations > 300 million.

7. **Indonesian** - The mother tongue of Indonesia. Over 300 million speakers.

8. **Bengali** - A language and a dialect. Over 279 million speakers.

9. **Russian** - A Slavic language with Greek alphabet > 258 million.

10. **Portuguese** - Spoken in Brazil, Portugal & several African countries > 230 million.

11. **Swahili** - Most spoken language in Africa. Over 200 million speakers.

12. **Urdu** - The official language of Pakistan > 170 million

13. **Japanese** - A defining language of a culture > 150 million

14. **German** - Official language of Germany > 140 million (maybe more)

15. **Punjabi** - The language of eastern India. Punjab > 130 million

16. **Vietnamese** - The official language of Vietnam >

17. **Javanese** - The language of Java. Indonesia > 85 million

18. **Yue Chinese aka Cantonese** - A Chinese dialect > 80 million

19. **Telugu** - Another language of India > 80 million

20. **Turkish** - Official language of Turkiye. Over 78 million speakers.

My name
is Michele.

PISA TOWER
PISA, ITALY
Mi - ke - le
Say my name
in Italian.

My name is Michae´l.

THE COLOSSEUM
ROME, ITALY
Mi - kha - ul
Say my name
in Latin.

My name
is Mikhail.

Mi - kha - il
RED SQUARE
MOSCOW, RUSSIA
Say my name
in Russian.

My name is Michail.

Mi - kha - el
THE
PARTHEONS
ATHENS,
GREECE
Say my name
in Greek.

My name is
Maikal.

TAJ MAHAL
AGRA,
INDIA

Mahy-kuh I

Say my name
in Hindi.

BONUS LANGUAGES

19. **Korean** - Official language of South Korea and North Korea > 77 million.

20. **Marathi -** Another language of India. Mostly Bombay > 74 million